Ken McCullough | *Dark Stars*

OTHER BOOKS BY KEN McCULLOUGH

POETRY
The Easy Wreckage (1971)
Migrations (chapbook, 1972)
Creosote (1976)
Elegy for Old Anna (1985)
Travelling Light (1987)
Sycamore.Oriole (1991)
Obsidian Point: A Triptych (2003)
Walking Backwards (chapbook, 2003)
Walking Backwards (2005)
Broken Gates, 2012

TRANSLATIONS
Selections from Sacred Vows
(bilingual chapbook of eight poems, English-Khmer
by Cambodian Pol Pot survivor, U Sam Oeur, 1996)
special bilingual edition of *No Exit*,
twelve poems, English-Khmer,
by U Sam Oeur, 1997
Sacred Vows (bilingual collection, English-Khmer,
of poems by U Sam Oeur, 1998)

PROSE
Left Hand (2004)
Crossing Three Wildernesses
(memoir by U Sam Oeur
co-written with Ken McCullough, 2005)

Ken McCullough

DARK STARS

Red Dragonfly Press

Copyright © 2017 by Ken McCullough
All rights reserved

ISBN 978-1-945063-11-4

Acknowledgements
The following poems have appeared in *Green Blade* (Plainview MN): 'While Seeing Dylan Perform in His Home State,' two sections of 'Coyotes, In Three Acts,' 'Gone Beyond,' 'Lost Chance,' 'The Hook, '64,' 'In Lieu of Flowers,' and 'Twilight in Hibbing.'

'Summer Vaccination' appeared in *Walking Backwards* (Blue Light Press. 1st World Library. Austin•Fairfield•Delhi).

Cover artwork: 'Open Studio,' 2015, Lithograph on Rives BFK paper, by Lisa Nankivil.

Coyote drawing by Ken McCullough

Designed and typeset by Scott King
using Warnock Pro (text) & Manuskript (titles)

Published by Red Dragonfly Press
P. O. Box 98
Northfield, MN 55057
www.reddragonflypress.org

"If it be your will
To let me sing
From this broken hill
All your praises they shall ring"

– Leonard Cohen, from 'If It Be Your Will'

Contents

Coyotes, In Three Acts 11
Coyote Tag 14
Starling Meditation 15
Corvi 18
Considering Hibernation 20
Gone Beyond 21
A Lifetime 22
Lost Chance 25
Twin 27
Twilight in Hibbing 28
A Citizen of Two Worlds 29
Trials By 30
Childhood, Mississippi, Mid 40's 32
Fall of '56 33
Eastern Shore, Spring of '57 34
How I Got My Summer Vaccination 35
Kiss My Capt. Video Decoder Ring 36
The Block, '62 37
The Hook, '64 38
On the Island 40
Early Peonies 41
Seeing Snyder Again in the 80's 42
Seeing Dylan Perform in His Homestate, 1998 44
On the Road 45
Rest Stop 46
Avec 48
Joey 49
Socket 50
In Lieu of Flowers 51
Fear Itself 52
For Mary Oliver 53

In memory of

Barbara Marie Midgely McCullough
1917-2016

Vernon Lewis Ashley/ "Sinkpe"
1916-2015

William Joseph Broz
1949-2015

James Thomas Harrison
1937-2016

Nancy Ann Evans
1946-2016

Scott McAfee Wright
1945-2016

Leonard Cohen
1934-2016

Raymond A. DiPalma
1943-2016

John Calvin Rezmerski
1942-2016

John R. Birkbeck, Jr.
1930-2016

Bernadette Scarani Mahfood
1942-2015

Maggy Irma Josephine Jacqmin
1947-2016

James Warren Northrup, Jr.
1943-2016

Mose John Allison, Jr.
1927-2016

Merle Ronald Haggard
1937-2016

Prince Rogers Nelson
1958-2016

James Alan McPherson
1943-2016

William Patrick Kinsella
1935-1916

Fidel Alejandro Castro Ruz
1926-2016

Jerome Silberman/Gene Wilder
1933-2016

Alan Sidney Patrick Rickman
1946-2016

Umberto Eco
1932-2016

Cassius Marcellus Clay, Jr
Muhammad Ali
1942-2016

Coyotes, in Three Acts

I watch our shadows exchange places.
Jupiter atop the tallest pine.
Something large out there in the pasture
makes the dog pace and whine.

    I.

I buried a coyote behind the garage.
My son and I had spotted it
on the shoulder of the interstate—
I pulled over, backed up and
popped the trunk. Poked it with my foot—
barely stiff. I grabbed its hind legs
in one hand and slung it in the trunk.
When we pulled up the drive
our dog came to greet us;
I opened the trunk and
her hackles rose—she growled
then moved away.
I lifted the coyote out—
maybe twenty-five pounds.
We looked her over. Just some blood
from one corner of her mouth, otherwise
a perfect coyote, the canines white
a variegated coat with musk
of wildness, her eyes gone empty.
I palpated muscles and tendons
of the left hind leg
and felt the speed and grace.
My son inspected her
stroked his hand down her neck
then I got the shovel.

II.

It used to be that a grandpa coyote ambled through the horse pen in mid-afternoon, but the seven horses never flinched. In winter I'd find tracks in the snow circling our house. One summer out the window at dusk I saw a fellow's silhouette listening intently to my son play Chopin on the keyboard. When my son was done, the fellow rose and loped into the pasture.

When spring was greenest but mosquitos had yet to swarm, wrapped in a blanket our dog slept on, I'd go down to the catchpond where there were beds galore. I'd hear them moving in the brush after sunset and now and then one would sit across the pond and watch me. Whenever they'd caterwaul I'd do my piss-poor imitation which amused them, I think. We lost two cats to them—Mickey, the best of the litter and two years later, Reggie, who had no fear of dogs; from our bedroom window we heard their frenzied attack. Since then we bring the others in at night.

I still go down there though we have a deer fence around the vineyard and they don't come in close anymore. The catchpond is outside the fence and skinned of vegetation. Between choruses of frogs I sit there in my dog blanket longing for their overture—to join their nip and jostle, my snout nudged in glossy fur under high tide of black sky and fireflies until the pack across the road sets in and we answer them...

III.

Three crows watch in silence. Bees sluggish.
We walk the path through leafless fruit trees.
The dog, a shadow of the coyote buried
ten years ago. The others dog the shadow.
Would we dare disrupt their symmetry?
Our shadow in the shadow in the shadow.

Coyote Tag
Wyoming

From the Gardner River bridge
    I spot a coyote loping the trail
      that parallels the river
  in the gorge below
Scanning the terrain
    I see a way I can scramble down
      to get in front of him
        if he doesn't hear or scent me
I lock the car
    then sidehill around a stand of trees
to a meadow
  that fronts the trail
      & squat in a cedar blind
After 15 minutes
     I conclude he's meandered elsewhere
  or scented me and made a detour
I follow the trail tip-toe
     to where it T's
  As I stand there
     left foot forward
 I look left and see nothing
   look right
  just as the coyote
     leaps through the corner of my eye
  and steps on my extended foot
as he races by
    without looking back
as if to say
  "You're it!"

Starling Meditation
for Lynn

1.

Mid-October—
   our ancient sugar maple
      still full of green leaves
    twists its twin trunks skyward
     a hundred starlings
    in the canopy—
     chortling rattling clucking
whistling trilling whirring sprattling
like a manic orchestra tuning up.
I see only their flitting silhouettes in the green
   except when six or seven blast, synchronized
 into the blue
  and another five or six return.
   A younger overreaching maple
extends a branch of golden leaves
  into a gap at the left of the old one
where a solitary crow
    muses in this haven
now and then preening breast feathers
or under its right wing
   listening to the entertainment.
    Of a sudden
they fall silent—
     a single rusty deliberate voice
  gives the signal to resume.
 A Fed-Ex truck rushes up the drive too fast.
Our yellow cat sits at the screen door listening, watching
   retreats to a patch of sunlight on the couch.
A single blue jay shoots into the lower canopy
     then exits just as swiftly.

The flock quiets again—
    then half of them bursts from cover
      with a boom
        to the north and circles back
          as if by remote control
        while the rest exit south to settle with others
      in what's left of the grapes in the vineyard.
        The solitary crow flies too
Cawcawcawcawcaw
Cawcawcawcawcaw

2.

I wonder what the starlings communicate—
   have they heard the scuttlebutt of the presidential debates
or of Jose Bautista's bat flip?
      Do they know of Starling Marte
  or Fayssoux Starling?
        Instantly they have disappeared.

It is quiet now after this half-hour cacophony
   but for the buffeted leaves
      that will soon enough be gone.
To the left our two old horses
      nuzzle water from the leaf-filled tank.
  A huge puffball guards the grave
        of our cat Mr. Black who died last winter
     at 15 years—
a loyal friend and familiar.
   The lone yearling deer has found
      a safe haven in the windbreak
and the scrub trees along the corral.

The blue jay is back
            with bravado—
free rein of the upper canopy
         and the last stations of the day.

Corvi

A spell of warm days
    unseasonable, no skin
of ice on the horse tank
    Two gangs of crows
veer through the treetops
    eyes black, eyes intent
on infiltrating
    the penumbra of darkness
inside the barn
they fear
    but never enter
They shine like dark stars
    until I raise my left hand
and the youngest of them falls
    almost to the ground
Outside the fence
    stench of a fawn
they've pulled the tendons from
    Can they hear my thoughts
see the hollow bones beneath my shirt?
    Last week I came upon
their congregation
    circled in the snow
the leader gurgling
    the others cawing, dodging their heads
in anger or agreement

West of Choteau, my uncle
    lived with a crow
He moved his body in crow fashion
    and spoke only with
gestures of his head

    Before the crow there was a woman
but she disappeared—
    just a pair of elk-hide slippers

Five days ago
    there was still black ice
under the snow—
    they tried to will me
to fall and crack my head
    but I could hear their minds
look down the hallways
    of their bodies
I hide things from them
    slide a stale muffin
under the heavy shovel
    a photograph
taken 50 years ago
    stuck in a cracked ceramic jug
Disconcerted
    they always find them—
a crow is a crow is a crow

This morning
    two black tail feathers
on the steps
    when I go to feed the horses

Considering Hibernation

If you could modulate the high drawl
a lame fellow emits, the keening
from an older sow, and begin a hum
somewhere in between, you might settle
down to the staple shunt of red sleep:
it wouldn't be hard, then, to parse grace.

Gone Beyond

The black rushes sway in tight formation,
a white-bellied hawk suspended overhead.
Summer's hand on fall, nibbling the quarry
in opalescent dusk. One is absent, one
immersed: your life, my loss. My eyes stutter
on the log bridge, on the fever of birds.
Our *sacra conversazione* over—
still, stilled as green flares on the horizon.
In perfidy, ingesting the evening.

A Lifetime

The novice hit the gong and the sound
reverberated through the leaves
my job was sweeping the paths, yours
washing the feet of the wise ones

I remember the sound of bells
on your ankles

I have met a few saints along the way
but missed some others because I was looking down

there was the village nearby
with another fifteen feet beneath it
and another down below that
and so on and so on
a hundred small houses
a childhood fallen in

when their husbands were in the fields
and they were not, their laughter was sweeter
yours among them

inscribing my poems on thick leaves
with a stylus—several dried that way
others faded and disintegrated

why was it when I walked out at night
something was always swaying above me
and when I swam

I sought the cave under the bank
and stayed there until you called me back

my fingers cracked and rough
but they remember fifty years ago
the smoothness of your skin
my tongue the taste of your lips
a neck that had never known pearls

you could read the smoke in the trees
low clouds suddenly over the cliffs
exactly where the swans would alight
how many would make it home

we made our nest
in that slanting farmhouse
beyond the village
surrounded by birds that appeared
nowhere else in our province

at the moment he was born
I felt something heavy fall away
and a green crystal take its place
your heart tighten
on seeing a king for the first time
no, really, a king

dogs have assembled on the promontory
and dangled worn ropes to the flagging sunset—
is this the start of the ending

here
where the nerves of nightfall are exposed
I can't even conjure your face
and barely remember you
in the winter bed

and then you were without form
grief unconscionable

the summer no visitors opened the gate

Lost Chance

Last year
in the foothills of the Bridgers
I spotted a man
a disheveled angel
down on his knees
in the glacier lilies
the delicate wild onions
his arms were bare
hair thin
clothes a patchwork
words... a song of sorts
came out of him
too faint to hear
it was June
snow gone
except where the sun doesn't hit
and carcasses had emerged
like remnants
of foolhardy expeditions
I edged closer
he was aware of me
but never looked up
one hand in an anthill
his mouth profoundly open
I knew not to look him
in the eye—I kept my eye
on the horizon, on a branch
with a small hawk
on a skein of lavender clouds
I began to make of the song

stones cracked open
but I was afraid to look
at what was inside
I could have touched the man
I was one step from him

Twin

From the time I was a kid
I saw my twin brother emerging
from a slit in a blasted oak
my exact double except
he had just one eye
the other sealed over
He'd give me halting advice
in a rough voice
I could barely understand
Sometimes he would put his hand
on my left shoulder
and cry softly from his good eye
In the last year or so
he's shown up
only in my dreams
He'll take my hand
and hymn me down the mountains
in a sweet gurgle
I remember
and lead me to the place
where his body sleeps

Twilight in Hibbing

The original town of Hibbing, Minnesota was founded in 1893. Shortly thereafter, iron mining began nearby, resulting in the largest open pit iron mine in the world. When it was determined that some of the deposit existed under the town, the Oliver Mining Company negotiated with the citizens to move the town (200 buildings) to a site two miles south, and, in addition, to construct several substantial civic buildings. This move occurred from 1919-21.Today, the mine is a tourist attraction, and visitors pass by the ghost template of the original town, where the streets and outlines of the foundations of buildings are quite visible.

Just a grid with a hatch of buckthorns
and an errant mockingbird. Sightseers
pass on their way to the mine, the town
a stereopticon mirage. Occasionally, a boy
on a bicycle disappears and years later
you hear him singing just before you
are called away. At the eastern edge
of the grid is a set of small boulders
arranged in the shape of a maple leaf.
Every year one of them gets taken away.
There are only three of them left now.
Every dusk from the limb of a red oak
an owl plops her casting in the stream.
She has the face of an eight-year old boy.

A Citizen of Two Worlds

I am a citizen of two worlds: one
with valleys and bluffs and birds circling,
green crops, golden grain insinuating the wind,
where neighbors wave and chat now and then.
The other, of people and gatherings and houses
on streets in rows, bands practicing for a parade—
echo of snare drum rim-shots and the bass
drum beat. Coffee shared at the sidewalk café.
And a third, where the shadows are deep
and all of us carry the smell of smoke.

Trials By

I

Purgatory is somewhere in central Missouri.
I was near there once on a cross-country drive
to visit my father's grave in Mississippi.
Took a wrong turn when I saw the shot-gunned sign
but my hackles rose and my instincts told me
to get back to the main road I'd been following.
A friend of mine had been in a commune down there;
a collection of domes and wheel-less school buses—
he said the bark and dry grass in winter seemed tinged
with dried blood and the air left sulfur in your mouth.
He told me his life turned inside out in that place.
I'd been to Purgatory, Colorado, outside Durango
and stood by the creek where five men disappeared
from Silvestre Vélez de Escalante's expedition
their bodies never found, but the magpies
warned me their souls were trapped and still active.

II

You were my migraine playing over and over,
poorly lit, in divers cockroach cities of the east,
cathedrals with steps too steep. I was not exactly
lost, but an immigrant who never learned the language.

Who can blame the ligature? the ligature itself
was not at fault. Lifetimes ago, a millennium.
A twist of hyssop at different points in the plot.
You had just been there but were never there.

I might make it to the surface with one more kick
then find myself in freefall with shattered wings,
I might put my shoulder to this rusty pendulum
and disrupt for an instant these aeons of failure.

III

The framework still resembles its intended purpose
but all the joints are compromised. When I stand
I almost sink to my knees and my head goes black.
Blood filled with detritus. When I look across a field
there's a network of shrubbery in each eye, masking
the trees in the distance. I read the phone book
with a magnifying glass, the numbers swimming into
different shapes in front of me, a sham Kaballah.
I used to have a steady hand and my writing swept
across the page, with drawings small and precise.
Now no one can decipher any of it, not even me.
In bed I have to imagine scenarios and sveldt bodies
of the past: louvered, hoovered, outmaneuvered.
Tinnitus, always there, as loud as the din of cicadas.
My hair is almost white, and there's not much of it.
George Clooney as my screen-saver: nolo contendere.
Will it be Schubert or sherbet tonight? I soldier on.
Forgive me if I turn the volume down to nothing.

Childhood, Mississippi, Mid-40's

You bring out the funk of black-eyed peas in me
with ham, some vinegar, dash of hot sauce
fresh cornbread crumbled in a tall glass of buttermilk
The fried chicken on Sunday after church
as only my father could cook it
greens with chunks of fatty pork, butter beans
the fried okra dusted with cornmeal
the grits, the sweet corn and sweet potatoes
Oh, Vardaman, the Sweet Potato
Capital of the World! where we
stopped for a Grape Nehi and a spotty bag
of boiled peanuts at Uncle Prince's filling station
You bring out my father's garden in me
that grew leafy and strong and plump and ripe
him standing among his peach trees
pruned perfectly
singing in his deep bass
You bring out Aunt Grace's lemon ice box pie in me
watermelon dripping down my chin
home-made ice cream
churned in that wooden bucket
And then church again and the women
singing high and a cappella
Later, the sweetness of honeysuckle
outside my bedroom window as I said my prayers
before my mother read to me
And then the fireflies. And the whippoorwill
all through the night

Fall of '56

Marty was back again from reform school.
On the way to Red Shield football practice
he'd tote two Budweisers in his helmet.
After practice, he'd retrieve them from his stash,
pop them with a church key and hand me one.
Skunk cabbage lingered from along the tracks.
In fading light with ghost-breath in the air
we'd retrace our steps to a possum on a limb
we'd pitch clinkers at until we knocked it off.
Then Marty'd veer into the webby light
of the alley behind his place, and I'd do
"Moonlight Gambler" in my head,
slip a Sen-Sen under my tongue.

Eastern Shore, Spring of '57

Two miles down from us, sump of The Manokin
that emptied in the Chesapeake. The roads
trailed off in a crush of oyster shells;
everything was brackish in that peninsula.
Our neighbors' voices slipped out like the tide
and a whiff of unwashed sex hung in the air.
She was three years older, the landlord's daughter,
a bona fide drop dead dungaree doll.
Once, as we got off the schoolbus, she not
so accidentally brushed her breast against
my forearm. All the way down our lane
I throbbed. In the evenings I could see her
silhouetted across the hazy beanfields.
My heart sank with Hank and Marty Robbins.
Train on the horizon, highway parallel.

How I Got My Summer Vaccination

In the summer of my sixteenth year I lived in my overcoat half the day studying geometry and tectonic deuteronomy and blonde girls with high heels and asses. I took classes in typing blood and other body fluids and played baseball in a baseball suit the rest of the time I wasn't holding up the centerpole of the universe. And one time when the nighthawks wouldn't let me sleep and lifting the weight of the world wasn't enough I took a job at a circus. The circuses came and went and I set them up and tore them down. Carousel parts, chinese red and thickly greased, gears for engines of torture from Bunyan's nightmares. Mildewed canvases, men with cigars, everything smelling of piss, despair and resignation. Objects constantly impaled my palms—filaments of giant bulbs, nails, blades of light spinning out of septic darkness. And the women waited in every shadow, painted designs on my chest and pressed against me. And the fat woman emerged from her trailer every night the same to feed her chihuahua whose front legs had been sawed off and she'd offer it some raw tidbit and its eyes would bug and it would tilt toward the plastic dish until she'd yank the dish away and the little wretch would topple forward on its face and kick its back legs like a frog and a round phlegmish laugh would roll out from her and she'd roll her eyes, thrust her hidden crotch at me, spewing red beans and rice. But in all those blackstrap nights my eyes never once left her face.

Suitland, Maryland
1959

Kiss My Capt. Video Decoder Ring
WASP vs. wasp, 1960

In the spring of their final term
the 6th formers figured out how to tie
thread around several wasps between their

thoraxes and abdomens without injuring them—
In effect they had them on leashes like pets,
making lazy tethered flights. Then they

pointed the aerosol can of Right Guard
deodorant and lit the spray with a
monogrammed cigarette lighter laughing

as they torched the creatures. Boys will be boys
will be men who became scholars and captains
of industry, role models for the millennials,

proudly served their country, voted with
their golden pedigrees, held and continue
to hold dominion over the dumb beasts.

But the ante is higher than they figured.

The Block, '62

We took Buck's brother Randy
to Baltimore's Gayety
for his sixteenth birthday
Blaze Starr the headliner
on loan from The Two O'Clock
ended her act on a couch that
enveloped her in smoke.
She was 30 then, but
the other strippers, old enough
to be our mothers, already
on the droop—on the eve
of silicone implants. I
still feel the drum the sax
the bump and the grind.
Old men with peckertracks
and pit band like a bad toupé,
halitosis of the emcee's jokes
between the acts.
You didn't let your hand
settle on anything
or anyone's on you.
It was a spackled world
between black and white
and too much blue.
Defunct now
and I no longer
frequent the likes, anyway.
Hoping, my friends,
none of us replace
the men with roaming hands
and dyed hair
like Ronald Reagan.

The Hook, '64

In Marcus Hook, in May
though it felt like the dog days
we were cruising
not following a Christmas star
starrus interruptus
no stars visible above The Hook
though Sirius slightly
and its faint white dwarf companion
It was the day the Nile flooded
and the surging Delaware Bay
the refineries
biting the air
We'd just left Blackbeard
holding forth at the T-Bar
King Twigg, prostrate on the stage
doing Ray's "What I Say"
humping the mike stand
and the skinny white guitarist
a goateed zombie
playing Malagueña with just his left hand
lights flashing in time
Shotgun Kelly on drums
A month later, Twigg showed us
token white boys
a grainy clipping: SHOTGUN KELLY
KILLED NEAR ALLENTOWN—his convertible
flattened beneath a Greyhound
Cannon our guide
with his red-faced guffaw
and downstate grin
led us to a dim bar
frequented by gypsies

We entered and as we did
one flashed the eyes of her breasts
whooped and I was drawn in
Cannon clutched my arm and said
go ahead and we'll find you in the morning
with your balls cut off
I slipped him my wallet
and went ahead
said I'll call you
and they left me there
and here I am today intact
so far, intact

On the Island

My son and I have a beer in the dingy tavern
I used to frequent, where the same tamed ferrets
sit the stools and conspire in thorazine voices
across from the store where I bought my groceries
and stocked up for springtime soirées by the muddy river
catty-corner from the decommissioned school
where I had my first imagined kiss, and my heart broken
it is now an upscale breakfast nook, a community theatre
and a boutique with expensive counter-culture baubles.
The #16 bus still whooshes by the same forbidden girls
in maroon school uniforms and white knee socks.

Early Peonies

   the peony buds
      and their very own
         army of ants
on maneuvers
     don't know tophats
        from tapioca
but a wind
    from the southwest
  they recognize

Seeing Snyder Again in the 80's

He's much the same:
    truckin' stride
        mountain goat demeanor
    Tibetan about the eyes—
        a feisty sprite

after his talk
    I come up to him
        in a coat & tie
    and Italian leather shoes
  —gray in my hair
        and paunch from cityside
    wheel of parentkarma

    introduce myself

& he cocks his head
    leans back a step
    and eyes me quizically

I say
  referring to the way I'm dressed
    "Yup, it's me, all right"

He fixes me with a glance
    And
        referring to his own getup
      (short patrician haircut
            [Bubbs Creek update]
      professorial reading glasses
    neat blue suit coat
        snappy old tie

             & buttondown shirt
        —still the earring   [diamonds, now]
      & still three humpbacked flute players
                          on his beltbuckle—)
    says
          "Yup, it's me, too!"
                with eye crinkle
                and gold tooth smile
    13:X:83

Seeing Dylan Perform in His Homestate, 1998

    sadsack abednego
        articulate harpo
      confederate general
            baked at 350°
       for fifty-seven years
I see you
    still nimble quick
        approaching your
     dogjowled dotage
       ruff ruff
   ruffled in Superior wind
if I could only
    ignite you from within
        if I could only
uncontort
    your borderland disdain
       if I could only
  point you past the dark refrain

On the Road

I am out running an easy grade
in a place way west of here
and the light bristles and brindles
and the countryside aches.
You appear, old friend,
loping from the other direction.
We stop and talk of the trail
up nearby Suce Creek
and I notice the light
spinning out of your eyes

Rest Stop
for Bob Love

Twenty Herefords graze facing Mecca
regiments of corn surround a silo
     morning glories garland the barbed wire
men laying asphalt in mid-August heat-stink
then you appear
in a field of soybeans
   along 53
as I head south from Superior
so I pull off the road
on a sand track
  down to the riverbank
    to pray:
Thank you for the sweetgrass
     you grew at your place
   within shouts of the North Fork
and thanks for the news
that the kids are doing well
    that Inez is her usual stellar self
 (we are all good here, too)
Thanks for news of your upcoming
 sojourn to the scant country
    in the north of Saskatchewan
May your canoes cut the water
 and the fish fry up
nice in the pan
  May there be berries galore
May this trip add years
 to your honest and steady life
and the trusty machine of your body
    stay master to the touch
of the musty machines you use

    May your knowledge of words
   continue, and may you distinguish
      all their costumes
And as for me
      May I stay a strong oak in the water
May my vision clear of these brambles and vines
May the fat on my soul burn away
      through my own hard work
and the smell of my *body lose that*
patchouli underwhiff
   I am still a trafficker in broken agreements
     from the outskirts of New Anywhere
   and I carry that obsidian scalpel you gave me
     in my life as a barber
I am running out of days, my friend
     I can only conjure so many more
Send me a message when you get back
   and I will be listening

Avec
for Galway

I know my death is up here, somewhere—
   my feet, in would-be prophet's moccasins
     will recognize the path—
the meadow opens
   sweep of tiny prayerwheels
     all yellow, white and periwinkle
a bear just leaving
   a mule deer's silhouette
 against slate-green shadows
   and back by a rivulet
 an old wickiup
   an old woman
  before a popping fire—
my heart leaps
    when I see her!
Help me to remember
   even just one song
    or syllable she tells me—
As I draw closer
  her eyes reflect the flames

Joey (2001-2016)
for Orion and Lynn

our beautiful yellow cat
   who spoke to us so eloquently
   always groomed my beard
     as he did his father
    and his siblings
and even inside
    his dog's ears
died yesterday

   even as he was dying
he smelled like fresh-cut hay

I wept and kissed his forehead
   then each of his pure white boots
   then curled him in a shoebox
     and placed him in the basement freezer
   until next spring
     when we'll bury him
under the lilac hedge
   next to his father

I will forever
   see his upright stripy tail
  cutting through the wildflowers
as he makes his way home

Socket

I know you are the one who wrote the book,
you, the one who always picks up the check.
When I heard your voice all my senses shook,
unlocked my chains, a bushel and a peck
of the rhymes lined up for the slaughter.
You were naked except for blue knee hose
on an island swirling in red water.
Today, ten years later, I dip my toes
in the sea. I should have known you were right,
always, as the pelicans fly in low.
I never wanted to put up a fight;
in your presence, there is no ebb and flow.
I gave in back then and am still giving.
Thank you for this blessing, for forgiving.

In Lieu of Flowers
for Mary Lynn, on Valentine's Day, 2015

I

Outside these windows in the darkest night
we hear a barred owl, not a nightingale,
incessant in our twisted old maple—
comfort to you, but harbinger to me.
The candle by the bed is guttering.
I hear you muttering in your sleep—
we both have dreams that almost wear us out;
then we wake, to a world stumbling in harness.
The light comes through the curtains, your eyes smile—
your toothy grin, sunny disposition
always fill every room you occupy.

II

Our house on the bluffs may someday crumble,
we'll let the heavy fences fall and rot.
The fires in our bellies will have banked
to a bed of embers, but still burn hot.
Across these fields we wander in the dark
the splash of stars, the velvet petals fall.
I faintly hear young Puck a-singing.
The shaggy heads of peonies, browning
at the edges, mined by ants, purple-blue,
misconstrue and slumber, too. I lived all
those years without you, and now another
life, but deeper, begins again today.

Fear Itself

> "...the only thing we have to fear is fear itself—
> nameless, unreasoning, unjustified terror...
> – FDR, inaugural address, 1933

Fear of your neighbor, who prays a different way
his face a different color. You cannot comprehend
his language. We put up a fence to keep the rabbits
out, the neighbor kids from the apple trees
but a high fence with shards of glass to keep
"The Other" in their place? And such a fence
that runs from sea to shining sea, from
Checkpoint Charley to Checkpoint Zebulon?
Fear that your model of Jetski will not keep pace
with the Jones's. Fear that your hairstyle, your hemline
will not be *de rigueur*. Seal the attic, bats might get in
exterminate the bugs, zap the flies, switch the DNA
of the mosquitos. Put the lepers in a valley
with Ben Hur's mother and sister. Fear of mice,
open spaces, tight spaces, crowds, failure, success,
immigrants, ptarmigans, grizzlies, of flying,
of mushrooms, of trees, of spiders, snakes,
the dark, dirt, germs, hermeneutics, nightmares
daymares, mares, invasive plants, invasive fish,
invasive leprechauns, identity theft, two left feet,
encryption, penetration, nuclear annihilation
all the icecaps gone, kaput. Just look in the mirror
if you really want to get a fix on what to fear.

For Mary Oliver

I have just re-read *White Pine*

        a spartan meal
                of ripe essentials

it reminded me
        to be

      I took my long
           and wintry poems

     out to the compost
to return them

and to wait, awake, for the gifts

KEN MCCULLOUGH was born in Staten Island, NY but grew up in Newfoundland, and has spiritual roots in the backcountry of Montana and Wyoming. He was adopted into the Miniconjou band of the Lakota Nation. Since 1996, he has lived near Winona, MN, where he has decided to 'make his stand." He is just completing his second term as Winona's Poet Laureate. McCullough is married to playwright Lynn Nankivil. He is widely published and has received a number of awards for his work. This is his second book with Red Dragonfly Press. McCullough has also collaborated with Cambodian poet U Sam Oeur, a Pol Pot survivor, on a bilingual edition of U's poetry, *Sacred Vows*, and a memoir, *Crossing Three Wildernesses*. A documentary, *Across Three Wildernesses*, was made about their work together.

www.ingramcontent.com/pod-product-compliance
Lightning Source LLC
Chambersburg PA
CBHW051717040426
42446CB00008B/934